Table

Temporarily Broken
The John Akhoian Story

Dedication

I am writing this book for my two boys, Andrew and Christian. I want them to know the struggles I went through to become the man I am today, and I want them to embrace the struggles in their own lives as stepping stones to make them the men I know they can be. I want them to learn to welcome all experiences, good and bad.

I am writing it for my life and business partner, Tamar, for never giving up on me, even though she had good reasons, with all I put her through. Thank you for not abandoning me.

I am writing it for everybody with whom I have worked. I am writing it for those that shared my life and still do. I love you all for what you taught me, and I am sorry if I put you through any hardships. Please, forgive me.

Memories are fickle. Multiple eye witnesses to a crime will describe it differently, yet the experience was real to every one of them. The mind fills in blanks and manufactures illusions that can appear genuine. I tell you this as a disclaimer because the stories in this book are as I remember them, but that does not mean this is exactly how they occurred. I am relying on my mother's memories and those of friends. So, if you read this and remember an event slightly differently than I tell it, please excuse me.

The other important thing to know is that a few of the names in this book are fictional. Some of these people are still alive, and I don't want to embarrass or humiliate them. I would also like to acknowledge Rudy Uribe for helping me put this book together. Without him, this project would not have been possible.

Preface

Who is John Akhoian? I often ask myself that question. I am the owner of Rooter Hero Plumbing, the largest privately owned plumbing company in California. I am an industry leader, entrepreneur, acquisitions specialist, investor, developer, and CEO. But is that who I really am? I don't think we define ourselves by the positions we hold or the money we make. I believe that we are the sum of our experiences, and to be honest, that scares the hell out of me.

The thing that frightens me most about writing this book is unearthing some of my darkest memories. I'm talking about remembrances shaded with guilt and filled with disgusting acts. Yet here I am, bringing everything to light. Many of the things I did were illegal and shameful, and I have told very few about them – until now.

The teenager and young adult you will meet in this book is not someone you would welcome into your home. You would never invite this person to Sunday dinner. The early "me," as you will see, did vile things.

But the purpose of this story is to show you that people can change and change for the better. I met good and bad people along the way. I served my time and paid a dear price for it, and fortunately for me, the good people had the biggest impact. The person "you would never invite to Sunday dinner" is now respectful, humble, and blessed with a beautiful family. When you get to Part II of this book, you will see how I have changed. I am far from being the person I want to be, but I am also not the person I was.

Christian, Andrew, I am happy to discuss anything you read in this book, but you will have to be the ones who bring it up. I thought I had locked some of these memories away. But I touched that first domino, and now I cannot stop the cascade.

Writing this book is important because it may explain why I sometimes act the way I do. Although I have changed, based on my early shenanigans, I should be dead or, at the very least, in jail.

Some fears are justified, and some are not. I learned that logically, working through phobias doesn't mean that I will successfully overcome them. Many fears have nothing to do with logic; they have more to do with events that have emotionally scarred me. Many of those scars are still with me.

A plastic surgeon can permanently remove a physical scar. I suppose the emotional equivalent of a plastic surgeon is a hypnotist who can help me forget the past, but forgetting is not what I want to do. Whitewashing my personal history doesn't make me a better person. I did what I did, and I must live with that. Do I have regrets? Absolutely! I took a stroll through hell as a teen, often bringing my parents with me. I need to expose the demons that frighten me to this very day.

One of my greatest fears is that these devils hide inside people I meet. I can't help but wonder if business associates, friends, or friendly competitors are just waiting to seduce me down that rabbit hole. As a result, I keep relationships light and superficial. Logically, I know that makes no sense, but it makes me feel secure.

My parents were not perfect. They made mistakes rearing me, and they did things that caused me to rebel against them and society. My parents are good, loving, flawed human beings who did what they thought was best. I'm not too fond of some of the things my father did, but I am not blaming him for my actions. Regardless of the challenges I faced as a child, I take full responsibility for my actions.

With all my love,
Dad

Part I

Regrets-The Early Years
A Walk on the Wild Side

Chapter 1
A Near-Death Experience and Abandonment

I have no recollection of my time in Armenia, save for the stories passed down by my parents. Armenia sounds like a wasteland governed by robotic soldiers who would do the government's bidding regardless of the cost to human life. America, on the other hand, sounded like nirvana.

When we moved to the United States, we lived with my paternal grandfather and his new family in a two-bedroom apartment. I was too young to remember that time, but I can't imagine it was pleasant for my parents. It must have been bittersweet because my grandfather was happy with his new family and here, my parents were living with them, but glad to be in America. My parents didn't speak a word of English, and they had to find a way to provide for my brother and me. My dad worked hard to gain our independence, and a year later, we moved to a place on Normandie and Sunset before finally settling into a one-bedroom apartment on Gordon Street in Hollywood, CA.

Our apartment had a swimming pool in the courtyard, and hanging around it was irresistible to a three-year-old; after all, we didn't have any pools in Armenia. I was often unsupervised as a child, and I loved dipping my toes in the water. One morning I stood too close and fell in. Pools didn't have security fences back then, and I didn't know how to swim. I immediately took in water and sunk to the bottom. A neighbor heard the splash and looked out the window only to see no one. She was sure she heard a splash, and she went to investigate. She saw me lying on the bottom of the pool. The woman jumped in, pulled me to the surface, and administered CPR. I must have been too young to understand what happened because, to this day, I do not have a fear of water. I am lucky to be alive, and as you will read later on, I have had several close calls with death.

By the time we moved to Hollywood, my dad's English had improved enough to get by. He did odd jobs and worked part-time as a mechanic. The building we moved into had ten units, and my parents took over as managers, which afforded us a discounted rate. My father quickly made friends with the tenants. As a three-year-old, it didn't matter where I lived. I didn't know a one-bedroom apartment from a three-bedroom house. But as I grew older and I saw where some of my friends lived, envy crept in.

That apartment where I spent thirteen years of my life represented some tough times. My parents slept in the bedroom, my brother, Abraham, who was five years older than me, slept in the living room, on the sofa. I think the sofa converted into a bed, but I wouldn't be surprised to learn that it didn't, and I slept in a single bed next to him.

One evening when I was five, I rolled out of bed, looked around, and realized I was alone. I was terrified. Had my parents been killed, or had they decided they didn't want me anymore? In my mind, it had to be one of those two choices, and neither one of them was good. My parents were gone, and I was alone. I am embarrassed to say that I soiled my pants and cried.

People today would look upon leaving a child alone in an apartment with distaste, but in 1977 it was a different world, and my parents did not think they were doing anything wrong. After the drowning incident, you might have thought that they would have kept me close at hand, but that wasn't the case. I was alone, and I sobbed until mom and dad walked in through the front door. It could have been an hour or five minutes; I'm not sure because time is distorted in my memory. My mother explained that they were visiting neighbors who lived two doors down.

Once I calmed down, mom cleaned my bottom and gave me a quick bath. My parents must have felt terrible. Mom explained that I was asleep, and they didn't want to wake me. I was never in any real danger, and they figured it would be okay to leave me alone for a few minutes.

On that day, part of me broke, and pieces would continue to fall off for several more years. From that day forward, I wet my bed every night until I was nine years old, and it drove my parents crazy. My father couldn't understand what was going on, and I was too young to understand it myself. It wasn't until years later that I put two and two together.

When my son Andrew was born, I swore I would never abandon him, and I went overboard. Like many parents today, we had baby monitors in every room, and we listened for any sound of movement or crying. Having the monitor meant I was always with him.

Many parents relax when the second child comes along because they have experience under their belt. Christian was born five years later, and I still felt the need to monitor him every second. This fixation with not leaving kids alone has created a generation of helicopter parents. The term suggests that parents are constantly hovering over their children. I hope this obsession doesn't implant a new fear that my boys will someday pass on to their children. Sometimes an over-correction can have a negative effect.

We lived in that tiny apartment for what seemed an eternity. It was too small for us to have friends over for playdates. Living in those cramped quarters became more and more difficult as my brother and I got older. Abraham was a teenager with no privacy, living with his little brother in a 500-square foot room. And to make things worse, to get to the bathroom, we had to go through our parent's bedroom. If my parents were asleep and we had to go to the bathroom, we would hold it because my dad was either tired or had to get up early the following day for work. Walking into their bedroom was invasive, and we never wanted to bother them. They never told us we couldn't use the bathroom; it was a rule we created in our heads. Sometimes I wonder if that also contributed to my bedwetting.

It took nine years, but dad finally realized that my brother and I were getting too old to live in that one-bedroom space. I don't know how he got the money, but he managed to buy us a three-bedroom house in North Hollywood. He paid 130,000 dollars for it, which was a lot of money back then. But at long last, we were out of that dreadful apartment, which reeked of poverty, fear, and poor report cards. I never wanted to go back. Occasionally, my parents would visit some of their old neighbors, and they would ask me to join them, but I would have nothing to do with it. I never wanted to see that building again.

You have to realize that I was sixteen and my brother was twenty-one, and we didn't have separate bedrooms. We started getting on each other's nerves and eventually found it easier to avoid each other. One of my biggest regrets is that my brother and I are not close, and I think those cramped quarters widened that rift. Abraham was going to college and would stay away as long as he could, and I started hanging out with my friends, which, as you will soon see, wasn't the best idea.

Chapter 2
My Introduction to the Dark Side

I was thirteen when I first met my brother's friend Hratch. He and Abraham were seniors at Hollywood High, and I had great admiration for Hratch. He had the school's highest GPA and was voted most likely to succeed. Hratch had good looks and brains, and in my mind, that was everything.

After graduation, my brother Abraham attended Glendale Community College, where he majored in drafting. Hratch, on the other hand, was majoring in heroin. As he partook more and more of this terrible drug, he and my brother grew farther apart.

I was in high school now, and I could see the changes in this brilliant young student. He wasn't the same guy I knew when I was in junior high. His demeanor changed, his personality changed, and I saw less and less of him. One day Abraham received a call from Hratch's parents. They hadn't seen their son in days, and they wondered if Abraham might know where he was.

Abraham and other friends went looking for Hratch but came up empty. Abraham learned that Hratch broke into his sister's home and stole her jewelry and later broke into his parent's home and stole their jewelry.

It's funny how your admiration for someone can linger in your head. I still saw Hratch as a role model, but when I had the chance to try heroin, I didn't do it.

I was nineteen when my brother told me he saw Hratch. He was gaunt, homeless, and begging for money on the street. This drug took an honor student and turned him into a criminal dealing in dark alleys, scratching to get a fix. Heroin had decimated this bright young man and turned him into a shell of the person I once knew. Abraham and I lost touch with Hratch's family, but I would assume he is dead from an overdose if I had to guess.

My dad and uncle were both mechanics and worked on cars. I became pretty handy with cars, and as you'll read later on, I used that skill to make money. My love for cars introduced me to Sam, who I still consider an electrical genius. When it came to cars and electronics, no one could touch Sam's skill level. Since we bought and sold cars, I would occasionally bring him a car, describe the problem, and Sam would immediately know how to fix it.

Sam had the Midas touch and was making thousands of dollars a week. Sam was so good; mechanics in the area would send him their overflow or send him their problem cars. But money was a problem for Sam, and he found himself spending it on speed. Methamphetamines are highly addictive, and Sam was unable to fight them off. There were nights we would be out late partying, and we'd drive by Sam's shop at two or three in the morning, and Sam was working on cars. We could tell he was amped up, and it looked as though he hadn't slept in a week.

Sam had money and eventually bought the corner lot where he had his shop. He owned it outright, and we learned later he lost it all. He refinanced the property to pay for his addiction and, like Hratch, ended up homeless and living on the street.

Another friend whose name I will not mention introduced me to cocaine. I hesitate to tell this story because this person is doing what he can to overcome his addictions, and for that reason, he has earned my respect and confidence.

Fat Hovo, who lived across the street from us in North Hollywood introduced me to pot Pot is legal now, but I'm not going to discuss the pros and cons of smoking it, but I will tell you about its effect on Fats. They say marijuana increases your appetite, and it was never so true as with Fat Hovo.

I remember driving through a fast food location once, and Fats ordered three hamburger combo meals for himself. He devoured the food before we got home. Fats was constantly high, and the pot gave him a voracious appetite.

Aside from the weight, the drug eventually made its way in other areas of Hovo's life. It slowly took its toll on his short term memory, ambition and energy. Hovo married and had two children but pot became more important than family. He became dependant on his parents for survival and remains a burden to his surviving parent. I am glad I never liked pot or my life story might have turned out like Hovo's.

Fat Hovo eventually died from a heart attack due to obesity. At the time of his death, Fats weighed in at over five hundred pounds.

Chapter 3
Dad's Near-Death Experience.

I was ten the next time I felt abandoned. Dad was a long-haul truck driver and, on that night, he pulled into a truck stop sometime around midnight. He was sleeping in his cab when he woke up with cold sweats and pain in his left arm. He later told us he felt sick, and it never occurred to him that he was having a heart attack. Despite not feeling well, he got behind the wheel of his big rig and hit the road. He drove for almost an hour before having to pull over. That's how tough a man my father was. The details are sketchy, but dad managed to get someone to help him, and they airlifted him to the nearest hospital in Tracy. It was fortuitous that someone stopped to help him. He had already gone more than two hours experiencing heart trouble. Even an eight-year-old knows it's serious when a helicopter is summoned to transport someone to a hospital.

We were in the Hollywood apartment when dad suffered this heart attack, and my brother and I woke up when we heard mom crying. She told us that dad was in a hospital and had a heart attack. She put us in our dilapidated Oldsmobile and drove us to Tracy, California. Mom drove six hours, mostly on adrenalin because she hadn't gotten any sleep.

There were no cellphones back then, so the drive was glum. All I could think was that dad was going to die or that he was already dead. No one spoke the entire time; Abraham and I sat in the back, and mom was alone with her thoughts in the front. She cried most of the way, which was exhausting and terrifying. No young man wants to see his mother cry. What she must have gone through is unfathomable to me, even to this day.

My dad had done irreparable damage to his heart by waiting so long to get medical attention. He would later suffer a second heart attack and survive it, but my fear of abandonment came to a head when he suffered his third.

I was seventeen and living in our house in North Hollywood. I had procured a job at a nearby Bally's Gym, working the juice bar for minimum wage. I wasn't making much money, but I lived at home rent-free and managed to save enough to buy a used motorcycle. Dad hated motorcycles, so I didn't tell him what I had done. You know the old saying, better to ask forgiveness than to ask permission.

I searched the classifieds until I found the perfect bike. When I say perfect, I mean it was cheap and not in working condition. Thanks to dad, I could fix almost anything. I hid the bike and worked on it when he was away on a haul. One of the good things about dad being a trucker is that I knew his schedule, and I could hide a lot of things from him.

Although I never told dad about the bike, he somehow found out. It could have been a verbal slip from mom asking him if I had finished fixing the bike. I'm assuming that's how it came down, but I don't know. The bottom line is – he found out. He didn't say anything about it, but he had a plan to teach me a lesson.

He went to the hardware store that fateful morning and bought a heavy gauge chain and a padlock. He drove to Bally's, saw only one motorcycle in the parking lot, and chained it up. I'm not sure what dad was hoping would happen. Had he expected me to come home and complain about what someone had done to my motorcycle, of which he knew nothing? Fat chance of that happening! I'm not sure what outcome my dad was hoping for, but it never happened.

I was mixing juices and power drinks when some guy came in yelling that someone had chained his motorcycle and that he was calling the cops. I had never seen such a commotion at the gym. Of course, he never did call the cops, he was just venting, and I remember how hard it was not to laugh in front of him.

A few of us figured that some of his homeboys were playing a trick on him, or maybe it was a jealous boyfriend warning him to leave his girl alone. Whatever the reason, we found it hysterical. We helped him cut the padlock and sent him on his way. He was snorting and cursing that he was going to get even with the bastard who did this.

After work, I walked into the house, and I remember my dad asking me how I got home. I thought it was an odd question, but I answered him straight away. "I walked," I said.

"It serves you right," he said, "buying a motorcycle behind my back."

"How do you know about the motorcycle?" I asked.

"Never mind how I know. You know how much I hate motorcycles, and you still went ahead and bought one. I'll drive you to the gym and remove the padlock, but you're going to sell that damn thing. Do you understand?"

"*You* put the chain on the motorcycle?" I said, "That wasn't my bike. Some guy was pissed off and almost called the cops." I remember laughing so hard that it must have been contagious because my dad started laughing too. "My bike doesn't run," I told him. "I'm still working on it."

Dad told me to get the bike out of hiding and bring it out so we could work on it together. I loved working with him on projects. He would tell me stories of the old country and give me advice I still use today. We mainly spoke in Armenian, for which I am grateful because it kept my heritage alive. This was our conversation that day, as I remember it.

"Hovik," he said, Oganes was my birth name, but dad called me Hovik, "If you learn to use your hands, you will never spend a day without work. There are educated people out there who can't use a wrench or hammer. They will pay handsomely to have someone do that for them."

"So, are you telling me that school isn't that important?" I asked.

"No, education is a beautiful thing. I am telling you not to rely on one gift. Learn to use your hands and your head, and you will be comfortable your entire life."

"I want to be a truck driver like you," I said.

"No," he was adamant on this point, "Truck driving is an honest profession, but just as the road brings you home, it also takes you away from your family. Get a job where you can come home every night. My biggest regret is that I don't spend enough time with all of you."

We worked on that bike for hours. It was a hot day, and I remember dad sweating profusely. I asked if he was okay, and that's when he clutched his left arm. I kept asking if he was okay, but he was unable to speak. He lowered himself onto his knees and then collapsed. I immediately knew he was having another heart attack. I performed CPR based on what I had seen on TV. I didn't have any formal training, so I'm not even sure if I did it right. I begged him to hold on until the ambulance arrived.

Mom called 911 and then came out and stood over us. I could hear her praying under her breath. It seemed to take forever for the paramedics to arrive. In reality, it was closer to six minutes. They took dad's vitals and administered proper CPR. We asked questions, but they ignored us and continued to work feverishly. The ambulance pulled away, with dad on a gurney. Mom told me to get in the car.

What I remember most about that day is watching the ambulance drive away. I know that seems odd with everything that was going on, but something seemed out of place, and I couldn't figure it out. I stood on the lawn as the ambulance turned the corner. Mom was shouting at me, telling me to get in the car so we could follow them to the hospital, but I didn't move. My mother's voice seems distant now, almost as if she was calling me from the clouds or a different dimension. Mom was frantic, and I just stood there. What was it about that ambulance that bothered me?

I always think of an ambulance driving fast with chaotic lights and sirens warning those in its path to pull over. The urgency rises with music that wears on the nerves on television, but it wasn't like that in real life. It wasn't like that at all. The ambulance carefully pulled out of our driveway. There were no lights or sirens, and my first thought was they treated us differently because we were Armenian. But it had nothing to do with our race or our zip code. There was no urgency because my father was already dead. I snapped out of my trance and kept this thought to myself. Mom was urging me to get in the car, and I obliged.

"I told your father to stop smoking and eat better, but does he listen to me?" Mom rambled on, blaming my father for his heart attack. I know she was scared, and that was her way of releasing anxiety. I didn't say anything because mom kept referring to dad in the present tense, which meant he might still be alive, so I held on to that thread of hope.

My life turned upside down on May 20, 1990. Dad's death is bittersweet because we spent the afternoon laughing and talking and working on my motorcycle, and it all came about because I had initially deceived him.

My boys and wife never met my father. They would have liked him, and he would have loved them. I wish so badly he had lived long enough to see the life I have today. I can only hope that my religious teachings are correct, and he is looking down on me with joy in his new heart.

Thirty years later, an event happened at work that gave me chills. I was at our corporate headquarters walking through the parking lot when I came upon a man lying on the pavement. Walter, who runs a shop in our building, had already called 911 and was administering CPR.

I flashed back to 1990, and I stood by, petrified, doing nothing. If someone were to ask me what I would do in a crisis like that, I would immediately say administer CPR, but the reality is we don't know what we'll do until it happens.

I speak fondly of my father, but I remember how angry I was when he died and left me. I want to say he left *us*, meaning my mother and brother, but I took it personally. To me, it was the ultimate abandonment, a kick to the gut, and I think about it a lot. My dad died at the age of forty-six, and he left his seventeen-year-old son to provide for *his* family. How dare he!

When dad died, it threw the family into chaos. There was a possibility we could lose our house, and I would not go back to living in that damn apartment. I had to find a way to make money and fast.

Chapter 4
My Fear of Poverty

When you are an angry teenager with no scruples making money is easy. At least it was for this eighteen-year-old. After my father's death, I knew I had to step up and care for my mother. You might wonder where my brother Abraham was at this time. He was in college studying drafting and doing drafting jobs on the side to pay for school. Abraham was self-sufficient, but he wasn't making enough money to support my mom and me. My brother is one of the nicest, most honest people you will ever meet. He is, to this day, kind and gentle, but the angry version of me didn't have time for nice people.

After my father's death, I was determined to take his trucking route, but my mother forbade me. She echoed what my father had told me about life on the road. With my father gone, we were hurting for money. Mom got a part-time job at a retail clothing store and sold dad's big rig for twenty-thousand dollars, which gave us a little breathing room.

I dropped out of school and needed to get a job. Mom lent Arthur, a plumber and family friend, ten thousand dollars to support his plumbing business. Mom isn't much of a business person, and she hoped he would pay the loan back with interest.

Now that Arthur had some money, he took me on as his assistant. Arthur was a plumber with little ambition to get rich. He reminded me of my father, who provided for us but had no desire to own a big house or a nice car. I owe him a lot because he taught me how to plumb a house, and I developed my love of plumbing from working with him. Although he would run small ads in the newspaper classified section, most of his clients came from word of mouth. Arthur was a conscientious plumber who took pride in his work – a trait he passed on to me.

There were no social media platforms back then, and there were no five-star reviews but had there been, he would have had an overabundance of business. Unfortunately, he never paid my mother back, and I still resent him for that.

Arthur and I worked Monday through Friday and took the weekends off. As he drove us around in his truck, I would see a lot of other plumbing vans from national companies, and I imagined they were making a lot of money working seven days a week. I tried talking him into getting a second van, then a third, and so forth, but again, he was happy with his little truck and had no desire to grow his business. The money I made as his assistant was coming from the money my mother had lent him. It was wrong in so many ways.

I hated living paycheck to paycheck and vowed never to live in poverty again. The fear of losing the house and moving back into small quarters had me looking for multiple income streams. I worked hard doing plumbing jobs for family and friends on the weekends. I worked five days a week with Arthur and two days on the weekends. The money was helpful, but it wasn't enough.

In the early 90s, Motorola came out with a mobile phone. It was large, bulky, and reminded me of a military walkie-talkie, but it worked, and Motorola was selling a ton of them. After a while, customers got upset with the high service charges. The business structure was somewhat like purchasing a home printer. The printer is inexpensive, but the ink cartridge is where they get you.

My friend, Tatul, was a hacking genius, and he learned to program the chip inside the phone so that the customer could have cellular service without the monthly payment. Motorola didn't realize what we were doing, or maybe it wasn't worth their time to deal with a couple of punk kids who were ripping them off. Tatul and I would sell these chips and tell customers they could have free cellphone service for a year. Programming these chips required no overhead, and we were making good money off of Motorola, who we justified, wouldn't even feel it.

Finding customers was easy. There was a large underground market, and we could trust these people not to turn us in for fraud because they themselves were also committing fraud by paying us. When you run a black-market operation, it's "hit and run." If the chip went bad or stopped working, that was too bad for the customer; we never left them a business card, mailing address, or other means to find us.

I now had three income streams. Uncle Armen was paying me during the week; I was plumbing on the weekends and selling Motorola chips to willing customers. But the fear of losing our house and my fear of poverty was deeply seeded. I needed to find yet another way to make money.

I was making 1,000 dollars a week with my different enterprises, and it was all in cash. That was a lot of money in 1992. I took some of it and went to the auto auction, where I could inspect cars before they came up for bid. I learned about the auction from my father and uncle, who took me with them on a few occasions. There were several cars I wanted to bid on, but I had a budget, and I stuck to it. Even as a teen, I understood the concept of profit and loss. I never got emotionally involved with a car because that could mean that I might overpay for it. It's the same in real estate. You never want to fall in love with a house because you'll end up paying whatever it takes to get it, and that's just not good business. I finally got the chance to bid on a car with muscle and sex appeal, and the price was right.

I won the bid and drove out in a Corvette that needed a lot of work, but I knew I could get it into shape with a small investment. Buying the Corvette taught me that I could easily buy cars, fix them, and resell them for a nice profit.

I returned to the auction and bought a highly sought-after Grand National. Buick built a limited number of these cars, and collectors were aching to get their hands on them. The law of supply and demand told me I could pay a little more for the car and still make a hefty profit.

And then, I came up with a plan that allowed me to outbid everyone at the auction. Bidders let me have the car because the price had gotten too high to make reselling the car profitable for them. I knew I overpaid for the vehicle, but as you will see, that was not a problem. I took the Grand National and drove it around for a month or two. Of course, I had to insure a valuable car like that, so I got the best coverage I could find.

One moonless night, I parked the car in a bad neighborhood and stripped it down. It was late, so I wasn't expecting any interruptions, but if a cop caught me, I would show him my registration slip and tell him the car broke down, and I was fixing it. There's no law against working on your car if it breaks down on the road. A friend, Hagop, helped me. We disassembled the car quickly and without incident. A few residents probably saw us stripping the car, but no one seemed to care in that neighborhood, and no one called the police. I stored the parts in Hagop's garage, and then he drove me home.

The following morning, I called the cops and reported my Grand National stolen. The police found my car stripped, and the insurance company paid up. I took the payout and waited for my car to come back up at auction. This time, I bought it dirt cheap because it was missing so many parts. Finding original parts for a Grand National was not easy, so no one wanted to bid on the car. It was an adrenaline rush watching my plan come together. I bought the car and towed it to Hagop's house. We still had the original parts we had removed and put them back on. I remember making a lot of money on that car…twice.

I hung out with a lot of crooks and thieves that negatively impacted my teen years. One friend, Ara, was a professional thief. By that, I mean he made his living breaking into cars, stealing car radios, and selling them on the black market. In the early nineties, Baker radios were in high demand and often found in high-end luxury cars like Mercedes Benz and BMWs. Ara's luck ran out one morning at 2 am when he broke into the wrong car. The owner had a gun and shot Ara in the back of the head as he fled the scene, killing him instantly.

Tatul, the same friend who could reprogram the Motorola phone chip, learned to reprogram debit cards, which turned out to be another gold mine. Tatul purchased a black-market hotel key machine, the ones the hotels use to program room key cards. Room cards are the same size and shape as credit cards. He tinkered with the unit and turned it into a device that could load money onto our debit cards. We took the fraudulent card to the Automatic Teller Machine (ATM) and withdrew the maximum amount of money; I think it was 300-dollars a day back then. Once we took the money out and the card balance was back at zero, Tatul would program more money onto it, and we would go back the following day and take out more cash. I doubt you could do that today, but in the early 90's it worked beautifully.

Not having money is a problem, and having too much money is also a problem. When you're nineteen and walking around with more money than the average person, it goes to your head. My teen years were the time when I needed my dad the most. I know he would have gotten me off the street and away from these illegal activities. But dad was gone, and it was open season on ripping people off, using drugs, and hanging out with the corrupt underbelly of humanity.

Today I consider myself a model citizen, thanks to my wife Tamar, who makes sure everything we do is above board and legal. Even though I am blessed with having a lot of money, the fear of losing it is still with me. It's a nightmare I can't seem to shake.

As I write this book, my company, Rooter Hero, has locations in California and Arizona and employs hundreds of people. I have a beautiful home in California, a Tesla, a Bentley, a Range Rover, and a Mercedes Benz. I don't tell you this to impress you, but I think the size of my house might have something to do with that tiny apartment in Hollywood. To this day, the thought of that room makes me cringe. As for the vehicles my wife and I drive, they are new and not stripped-down versions from an auction.

I paid a heavy price for the things I did as a teen. I have been in jail four times and once in Juvenal Hall, but this is only a small part of my troubled youth.

Chapter 5
Jail Time

The year was 1991. I was in a car with my friend Andre in front of a pool hall. We weren't doing anything illegal, just sitting and talking. Andre was heavily into drugs, liked to smoke Kool cigarettes laced in Elephant tranquilizer and PCP, and he had a couple hidden in his cigarette pack. The effect of the laced cigarettes was out of this world. When I partook, I felt invincible and numb at the same time. The drug would give me these Alice-in-Wonderland-like hallucinations, where inanimate objects would come to life and talk to me. I found out later that if I had not broken the habit, I could have lost my vision, or at the very least, impaired it badly.

As I write this chapter, Andre is out of prison for killing Hagop (you'll find out how in a later chapter) and is legally blind because of the drugs. We were smoking regular cigarettes when a cop pulled up and told us he smelled drugs. I doubt he smelled anything, but that was enough to give him probable cause, so he searched Andre's car. He took Andre's cigarette pack from the glove box and found two drug-infused cigarettes. He placed us in handcuffs and hauled us away for possession of drugs.

I can only imagine what I put my mother through. Time after time, she bailed me out, and I never seemed to learn my lesson. I went through that period in my life, unaffected by injurious consequences. It sounds like an oxymoron, but incarceration was the price of freedom, and for me, freedom meant not following the rules.

***

The next time I went to jail, I was with my friend, Garo, who owned a beautiful slant nose Porsche. We felt like rock stars driving in that car. It was a real head-turner. One summer evening, we were at a stoplight in Hollywood when another vehicle pulled alongside. Garo had the music blaring, and this beautiful girl in the other car looked over at me. We made eye contact, and I flashed her a smile. Her boyfriend must have gotten jealous because he honked the horn and asked me what I was looking at.

I flipped him off, and Garo laughed. Then I remember blowing his girlfriend a kiss. The boyfriend flipped me off, so I pulled a cassette out of the car stereo and threw it at his window. It must have hit at just the right angle because the window shattered. The guy ran the red light speeding away, and I yelled at Garo to follow him so I could kick his ass. "You're not going to kick anyone's ass," Garo said, "you already scared the shit out of that guy. Besides, we're late for dinner." We were meeting friends at Benji's restaurant in Glendale, and I can't believe that Garo was the one who convinced me to chill out and enjoy the rest of the night.

We sat down to dinner, and Garo convinced me to tell everyone about the incident at the stoplight and how I broke the window. That's when we heard sirens outside.

Two patrol cops walked into the restaurant. One spoke in a loud voice. "Whose red Porsche is parked across the street?" he asked.

Garo panicked; he figured someone had broken into his car or maybe keyed it. "That's mine," he said, "Is there a problem?"

"Yeah, there's a problem. We got a call of road rage, and your license plate came up. Who was in the car with you?"

Garo turned and pointed at me. "This guy," he said. Everyone at the table laughed. I held both my arms out in front of me as if to say; I surrender, handcuff me. Everyone laughed even louder.

"You're both under arrest." The cops grabbed both our arms and cuffed us. Our friends stopped laughing and began harassing the police.

"This is bullshit," someone yelled, "They didn't do anything. They've been with us the whole night." Someone else grabbed a water glass and smashed it on the floor for dramatic effect.

"You want to join them?" the cop asked. Our friends got quiet, and we did the perp walk out of the restaurant. Once my dad passed, I had become the alpha male of the family, and I could do whatever I wanted, and nobody could tell me otherwise. I was entirely in control and very much out of control.

***

In the late eighties, I hung out with members of Armenian Power (AP). I didn't join the gang, but they knew Hogop and me and treated us like honorary members. AP thought they were a pretty tough gang, but there was a rival gang and they were scary.

This other gang started as a Central American gang and quickly escalated to a criminal organization, and they hated Armenian Power. They murdered two AP gang members in the ensuing weeks, and AP was determined to get even.

A month went by without AP taking any action, and I thought everyone had forgotten about avenging their friends, but I was wrong. Hagop and I were going to grab some burgers when we got a call from Crazy Vatche. Vatche needed a ride and asked if we could help. His name should have been the first tip-off that this was the wrong person to be with. Vatche was an outspoken AP member, and we didn't really know him, so it was surprising when he called me. To this day, I don't know how he got my phone number.

Vatche lived in the worst part of Hollywood. Drug deals were going down on almost every corner, homeless were sleeping on the sidewalks, and trash littered the streets. Vatche lived in a four-story apartment building, and we couldn't wait to pick him up and get the hell out of there. He was waiting on the curb wearing sunglasses, a bandana, a trench coat, and expensive athletic shoes.

As we pulled up, Hagop said, "There's something not right with this dude,"

"He's AP," I said, "he's cool."

"I think we should keep going," Hagop said, "He looks like he's ready to kill someone."

"Why," I said, "because he's wearing sunglasses at night?"

"Yeah, "Hagop said, "and because he's wearing a trench coat and it isn't raining."

"If we don't give this guy a ride, we'll never hang out with AP again. He'll tell everyone we stiffed him. I don't want this guy hating us."

I should have trusted Hagop's instincts, but I ignored his warning and pulled up to the curb. Vatche got in the back seat and scooted to the middle so he could see us both, "Where are you guys headed?" he asked.

"We're gonna grab some burgers," Hagop said.

"No, we're not," Vatche said, "We're gonna cruise Hollywood Boulevard."

"But we're hungry, and cruising will take hours," I said.

Vatche pulled a sawed-off shotgun from under his trench coat and made sure we saw it, "We're gonna cruise Hollywood Boulevard," he said emphatically, "That gang killed two of ours, so we're going to kill four of theirs."

Hagop gave me an 'I told you so' look. Sure, we had done some illegal stuff, but we had never killed anyone. We were scared, but you don't argue with a guy holding a shotgun. Hagop and I looked straight ahead and didn't make eye contact with Vatche or each other. When we got to the boulevard, the cruisers were in full force. The street was alive with music, pretty girls, and expensive cars. Movie marquis lit up the boulevard, and street performers were having a good night.

Vatche scooted over and sat behind the driver—me. When someone says they want to ride shotgun, they mean the front passenger seat. The shotgun side of the car had just shifted to the position behind me. If Vatche fired the shotgun while we were in the car, it would deafen me.

"Let me know if you see anyone wearing black and blue bandanas," Vatche said. The colors, black and blue, were the gang colors. We uttered a sound of acknowledgment, but our voices had gone up two octaves. We thought we were pretty tough until a guy with a shotgun got in the car.

We cruised for over an hour, and a couple of times, we thought we spotted them, but we didn't tell Vatche. After a while, I remember saying, "Well, I guess there's no one to shoot tonight. Let's get something to eat." which I regretted as soon as I said it. Vatche leaned over and whispered in my ear, "We go home when I say we go home."

"Yeah, John," Hagop said, "we don't go home until we kill four of those bastards!" Hagop was trying to get on Vatche's good side, but it only made me look worse.

Because of the bumper-to-bumper traffic, LAPD had foot patrols on the sidewalks and equestrian units moving between cars. Any other tactic would have been useless. The police presence didn't seem to bother Vatche one bit. He sat behind me with the shotgun in his lap, ready to shoot the first gang members he saw.

We worried that if something went down, there would be no way out. Vatche was no tactical genius and hadn't thought of an escape plan. Later I found out he did have an escape plan; it just didn't include us. When we cruise, we are virtually not moving. If we needed to make a quick getaway, there weren't many options.

"There! Over there, I see two of them," Vatche said. "I going to kill those mothers." He started to open the door when I stopped him – "Vatche," I said, "Think about it. If you kill those two guys, you won't be able to kill anyone else. The cops will be all over you. Why don't we wait until we see four guys in a car?"

"You're right, kid," he said, "We have to find a car with four of those bastards."

I managed to prevent the killing of two people, but I didn't know for how long. I got the feeling Vatche was willing to wait as long as it took, and as I had already learned, there was no going home early.

An equestrian unit came up alongside us, and I was sure they would look inside the car and see the shotgun on Vatche's lap, but the cop kept moving. "That was close," Vatche said, "those pigs are dumber than their horses."

We cruised for another forty-five minutes, and I tried to break the silence by turning on the radio, but Vatche quickly put an end to that. Up ahead, we saw a convertible with four gang members. Hagop and I looked at each other but said nothing. They were twenty yards away and would soon be in Vatche's sight, and this time, there was nothing I could do about it. We were crawling along getting, closer to our targets.

"There they are," Vatche said, "you idiots are useless. Didn't you see them?" It was a rhetorical question because he didn't wait for an answer. Vatche jumped out of the car. "Wait here," he said. As if. My heart rate jumped. This was it. I wasn't sure what Vatche would do, but if he shot someone, jumped back in the car, and told us to take off, we would be screwed.

Vatche ran down the median and opened fire on a convertible. One of the guys managed to get off a shot. I don't know if they winged Vatche or not. The sound from the blast was deafening, and people panicked. I remember girls screaming and cars rear-ending one another trying to escape, but there was no way out. I looked around and saw cops running after Vatche. As luck would have it, we were at an intersecting alley. I drove on the sidewalk, made a quick right turn, and drove away from the crime scene.

Vatche ran down the alley in the opposite direction. The cops followed him, but he was putting those new sneakers to good use. As I mentioned earlier, Vatche had an escape plan; it just didn't include us. To this day, I don't know if he killed anyone, but I'm guessing he did. As for the cops, I don't know if they caught up with him, but we never saw Vatche again. As for Armenian Power, we were done with them and their crazy ways.

31

Months after the shooting, Hagop and I were still nervous that someone might have seen Vatche jump out of our car. We didn't shoot anyone, and even though Vatche commandeered our vehicle against our will, I'm not sure a judge would have seen it that way. We kept looking over our shoulders, wondering if a swat team would show up at our house, but fortunately, they never did.

***

My third and fourth times in jail were due to road rage. I was so angry back then that if someone cut me off or flipped me off because I did something to them, I would go bonkers and chase them down with the intent to scare the crap out of them or to do them bodily harm. I think back to those days, and I can't imagine how scared the people I pursued must have been.

There was one other time when I had to go to juvenile hall and appear before a judge. I felt that I had put my mom through enough hell, and I wanted to give her a break, so I asked my aunt, who was visiting from Armenia, to sit in for my mother. I laugh at this story now, but back then, it was no laughing matter.

My aunt agreed, and we took my 280Z to my appointment. My aunt didn't know a courtroom from a library, and she thought all she had to do was sit and wait for the proceedings to end. I lied to her about why I was there. My aunt didn't speak a word of English, so she just sat on one of the benches looking around.

"Mrs. Akhoian," The judge said. My aunt ignored the judge; after all, her surname wasn't Akhoian.

"Mrs. Akhoian," the judge said sternly. Again my aunt ignored him. It didn't take long for me to figure out that bringing my aunt was a bad idea.

"My mom is deaf," I said, hoping that would explain her indifference. I could have said she didn't speak English, but they would have called in a translator. I thought I had outsmarted them.

The judge looked at me, "You will speak only when spoken to. Is that understood?"

"Yes, judge," I said.

That's when the judge called for someone to speak to my aunt in sign language. I remember she was a skinny woman with white hair. She stood in front of my aunt and signed the judge's message. *"Mrs. Akhoian, do you agree to take charge of this juvenile, and will you do everything you can to keep him out of trouble? Including complying with a nine o'clock curfew?"* My aunt, who had no idea why this woman was making all these hand gestures in her face, looked at the woman uncomprehendingly.

The judge pounded the gavel, and my aunt flinched. "Mr. Akhoian," the judge said. "This woman is not deaf, and I doubt she is your mother. You have made a mockery of this courtroom." The bailiff took me away in handcuffs.

Chapter 6
Guilty and Guilty by Association

A few times, I got blamed for things I did, and a few times, I got blamed for things I didn't do. I guess there are times when you are guilty by association, but that didn't slow me down.

My dad was the disciplinarian in the family, and I was always fearful that I would get caught doing something wrong. The first time I got in trouble by association was when I was in junior high, and my buddy, Hagop, gave me a call. We were fourteen and dating two girls who were best friends.

"Hey, John," Hagop said, "my dad's gone for a couple of days, and he left his car keys. Why don't we jump in the car and take the girls out in style?"

"I'm getting ready for my guitar lesson. I can't go right now," I said, "my dad will get pissed." Learning the guitar was not my idea of having fun, but my parents thought it would be good for me. My parents didn't have a lot of money, so music lessons were a luxury.

If I had respected my parent's opinions more, I wouldn't have ended up in so much trouble. I called my music teacher and told her an emergency had come up, and I had to cancel. Of course, my father would find out later when he had to pay the invoice, but at the time, I didn't think it through.

"I'll pick you up in five minutes," Hagop said.

The car wasn't anything special. It was an old Buick sedan, but when you're 14-years old, any car is special. We pulled up to the house, and the girls were impressed. They jumped in, and we went for a joy ride. I still remember the look on Hagop's face as he drove around. He was a big man with his girl, Zarmine, at his side.

I sat in the back seat with my girl, Lena. We were having a ball as we drove around Hollywood. Hagop stopped at a hamburger stand, and we grabbed some lunch. It was one of the best days of my life.

On the drive back, a black and white pulled up alongside. Here we were, two fourteen-year-old boys driving an old Buick and it didn't take a genius to figure out we didn't have dri er's licenses. It took just one wave of the policeman's hand to pull us over.

"Whose car is this?" the policeman asked.

"It's my dad's," Hagop said.

"License and registration."

"I forgot my license at home," Hagop said. Zarmine snickered, knowing he didn't have a license.

The cop didn't appreciate Hagop's attempt at humor. "All right, get out – all of you. We're impounding this car. Tell your father he can pick it up at the tow yard."

"But how are we supposed to get home?" Hagop asked.

"Not our problem," the cop said. When LAPD cops are in patrol cars, they never drive alone. They always have a partner with them. They were willing to let us walk home, but they showed more concern for the girls.

"Ladies, how far do you live from here?" The second cop asked.

"We live at the end of the block," Lena said.

"I'll escort you home while my partner waits for the tow truck." The girls knew they would be in trouble when a policeman walked them up to the front door. Their parents grounded them, and they shunned us at school. We never went out again.

"Officer," Hagop said, "If you let us go, I promise I'll take the car straight home." The policeman ignored his request and wrote something in a notebook. We were screwed, and we knew it.

On the walk home, Hagop turned the tables on me. He told me he would tell his dad that I was the one who forced him to take the car. "If my dad knows it was my idea," he said, "he'll kill me."

"If my dad thinks I had something to do with it," I said, "he'll kill *me*." We argued back and forth, but in the end, Hagop got his way.

Hagop's father bought the story and forbade him from hanging out with me. It wasn't long before word got back to my father that I had stolen a car. I should have preempted the rumor by telling dad the truth because the story he heard was a lie. I was grounded even though I denied stealing the car.

Hagop's father didn't know the car was missing when we were pulled over and therefore never reported it stolen, so when I tell you it was a "stolen car," I want you to understand that it was Hagop's father's car. Still, we were driving it without a license and permission. Hagop and I were lucky the cops didn't arrest us.

***

Once my dad passed away, Hagop and I hung out secretly. I would spend hours with him, and there were several times I had to sneak out his back door when his dad came home unexpectedly. It was nerve-wracking sneaking around all the time, but Hagop was a good friend.

I remember one day when Hagop stole some guy's motorcycle. He painted it to make it look different, but he didn't change the license plates. I didn't know it was stolen, and he let me ride it a few times. We were nineteen at the time, and I was already heading down a destructive path. Hagop hid the motorcycle in the garage. His father didn't know about the bike, which was similar to what I had done with my father.

My motorcycle story ended tragically, with my dad dying while helping me repair it, and Hagop's story ends tragically as well. He was on his bike one day when a cop hit his flashing lights. Instead of pulling over, Hagop ran because he knew he was on a stolen bike. To this day, we don't understand why they were stopping Hagop. Had it been because they spotted the stolen license plates, or was it because he was breaking traffic regulations? It didn't matter. Hagop panicked and took off.

The high-speed chase went through the streets of Glendale and moved to the northbound Golden State Freeway. Hagop wove in and out of traffic, a precursor of today's high-speed chases. He increased his speed until he topped off at 110 mph. I can't imagine what Hagop felt when he broke the one hundred miles per hour mark. At that speed, your reflexes can't compute what's ahead. You're low to the road, and the noise from the muffler interferes with your senses. When you finally spot a problem, it's too late.

An imperfection on the freeway's surface, imperceptible at normal speeds, raced towards Hagop. It was a bump, possibly caused by a former earth tremor, or perhaps it grew from the tens of thousands of heavy trucks that drove across it, compressing it into a road hazard. The bump ran across three lanes, and it moved like a concrete tsunami. It approached Hagop at 110-mph, and there was nothing he could do to avoid it. The bike hit the bump and catapulted Hagop a hundred and seventy feet through the air. He slid and toppled another two hundred feet on the rough pavement, ripping his skin and shattering his bones. They tell me it was gruesome. Officers rushed to his side, but he remained unconscious. California Highway Patrol officers closed the freeway until paramedics arrived.

Hagop survived but was in a coma for weeks. Once he woke, he told me he remembered letting go of the handlebars and flying through the air. He told me he was surprisingly calm. Maybe when the time comes, the brain shuts down the fear button and allows us to accept the inevitable. He remembers floating through the air in slow motion. I asked him how hitting the pavement felt, but he told me he didn't remember any of that.

With his legs shattered and organs damaged, Hagop underwent several surgeries. The surgery on his brain was the most delicate and required the implant of a metal plate. He was never the same. I visited him at the hospital when his dad wasn't around. It was hard watching him recuperate. It took over a year of physical therapy just to learn to walk again. Once recovered, Hagop made up for lost time. He played around and got a girl pregnant. He had no intention of marrying her, but his father forced his hand. I think his father's control fostered Hagop's rebellious nature.

Hagop was out of commission for so long after his accident that I started running with a different crowd, and we didn't hang out as much. But he still had a wild side, and his new family was holding him back. He told me he was suffocating and needed to get out. He called and asked if I wanted to party. I hadn't seen him in a while, and I thought it sounded fun, so I told him yes.

My mom needed some medication and asked if I would pick it up for her. I told her I was going out and I would do it tomorrow. She had heard these excuses before, and she knew I would never get her meds. I saw a tear slide down her cheek, and it got to me. She made me feel like an unloving son, and that had never happened before. Whenever my mother cried, it did not affect me, but this time it was different. I called Hagop and told him I had an errand to run for my mother, and I couldn't go out with him. Normally I would be upset with my mother for stopping me from going out, but running that errand saved my life. Had I gone out with Hagop, I would be dead.

This was the second time I dodged death, and I am sure I was spared for a reason.   I wasn't very religious as a youth, but I convinced myself that God had a mission for me as I matured.

Hagop had to get out of the house, with or without me. He got in his convertible, picked up Andre, and drove to a third friend's house. They partied heavily until about two in the morning. Hagop was dumb, drunk, and could barely stand. On the other hand, Andre was still able to walk and believed he was okay to drive. Andre staggered out the door with Hagop hanging on his shoulder. When I tell you I'm lucky to be alive, I'm not kidding.

Most people drive slowly when drunk, but Andre had a heavy foot. The convertible top was up as he headed east on the 118 at Balboa, going more than 100-mph when he hit a bump and lost control. It was eerily similar to Hagop's motorcycle accident. Andre wasn't wearing his seatbelt, and his body ripped through the canvas top like a projectile landing on the pavement. Hagop, on the other hand, was strapped in. His head took a beating as the car tumbled over the embankment. The plate in his head jostled about, and they say he died before the car stopped rolling. Andre survived the accident and wound up in prison for vehicular manslaughter.

I had just lost two of my friends. One was dead, and the other in prison. That should have been enough to convince me I was heading down a deadly path, but it didn't. I attended Hagop's funeral and heard the pastor say all these great things about him and knew it was bullshit. When someone dies, they say good things about that person, whether he was good or not, so I rationalized why bother being good.

Something about my dad's passing had set me free, and I don't mean that in a positive way. The disciplinarian in the family was gone, and I had no one to fear. I was unbridled and free to do whatever I wanted, no matter the cost.

In Part II, you'll see how my rage frightened my little boy and almost killed my mother-in-law.

Part II

My Ancestors –Their
Struggles
My DNA

Chapter 7
My Maternal Grandparents

Russia: At 3:00 am, an intense pounding roused my grandparents from a deep sleep. When my grandfather, Pasha, opened the front door, he saw one of Stalin's men pointing a machine gun, and he thought he was dead.

My maternal grandparent's life was about to be uprooted, and the government they despised would take everything from them – my grandmother, Rael, was pregnant with my mom, and this day would test her strength and her faith.

"Gather your belongings, "the soldier said, "You're leaving."

A neighbor told the authorities that my grandfather was a dissident who was against communism and who was against the Soviet Union claiming Armenia as a colony. In Russia, any citizen who disagreed with the government was exiled to Siberia. My grandparents and their two children, ages three and seven, gathered what they could fit into a suitcase and were driven from the little shack and home that they had built. It was made from dirt, mud, and stones

Soldiers prodded Pasha and Rael with machine guns into a livestock transport train and packed them in like the animals before them. The boxcar had no seats, windows, beds, or bathrooms, and the stench from the stagnant air was unbearable. Fifty dissidents crammed into the railcar for the seven-day trip to Siberia. The travel conditions were deplorable, and several of the women, including my grandmother, got ill. The living space stunk with sweat and feces, and the only place to defecate or urinate was in the corner of the boxcar. My grandfather knew the conditions were inhumane and realized it was a matter of time before people got sick and died.

Grandfather Pasha crawled around on his hands and knees and found a weakened floorboard. He and several other men removed it so the passengers could use the opening as a toilet. The only privacy afforded the women was to have blankets held around them while using the "facility." As my grandmother told me this story, she spoke of the passengers' gentleness and respect for one another. There were no fights among the men, and the women huddled to provide conversation and comfort in the most intolerable conditions.

My grandfather's toilet hole allowed feces and urine to exit the train, and it let fresh air into the boxcar, but the tight confines increased the sound of the wheels on the track to eardrum-shattering levels. At specific stops, the soldiers would slide open the doors, toss rotting food into the car, and then slide them shut, allowing a short interaction with sunlight. The passengers scrambled for the food, and in a show of unity, gave it to the women first. The dissidents treated each other with respect, and they distributed the food in an orderly and equitable fashion. Fruits and vegetables sustained everyone until they arrived at their destination. Little did they know what a delicacy those rotten fruits and vegetables would be.

The passengers spent seven days in the dark, enduring the infernal rhythm of the wheels on the tracks and the wails of crying children. Rael, my grandmother, remembers a few of the women getting sick with anxiety. Some of these women cried hysterically with the pain of not knowing what was to become of them.

Instead of comforting these women and reassuring them that everything would be okay, the men slapped them until they regained composure. It seems cold and uncompassionate, but it was how they handled things back then.

Siberia is a frozen, desolate wasteland known for its long, harsh winters. The northern tip borders the Arctic Circle, and the average temperature in January is minus thirteen degrees Fahrenheit (-13F). In the summer months, the weather can reach a high of sixty-five degrees (65F).

When the train pulled into the Siberian station, the soldiers took everyone to a twenty thousand square foot warehouse. The families lived there for a short time before being told to leave and build their own shelters. They were allowed to build on a piece of land that a rat wouldn't inhabit. They used tools and nails abandoned by those who tried to build before them but didn't survive the winter. The men worked long hours building makeshift homes that proved almost uninhabitable when winter finally came. Mother remembers when a snowdrift blocked the front entrance to their shack, and they could not leave. Grandfather put his shoulder to the door and pushed, but the snow was too heavy and stacked too high. The door didn't give an inch, and Pasha worried that if he hit the door too hard, it might splinter, letting an avalanche of snow into their living space.

Mom and her family sat in the cold and dark, wondering if they would die in this makeshift coffin. Eventually, the men of the village cleared a path to my grandparent's door. Snow drifts tend to build on the windward side of the storm, and some of the other shacks had their doors on the opposite sides allowing the residents to get out. Pasha joined the men to clear other homes of snowdrifts, and unfortunately, they lost a few people to the elements.

Farming in Siberia is virtually impossible, but the community grew some vegetables while trapping chipmunks and small rodents for protein. The women cared for the children, cooked, and made quilts to survive the winters. Mother tells me that when things got particularly tough, they would eat dirt because it, at least, had some nutrients.

As far as the Soviet Union is concerned, my mother is a phantom. She has no birth name, hospital, or attending physician on her birth certificate because there is no birth certificate. She is unrecognized by the government. This girl survived seven of the harshest winters Stalin could throw at her, and despite it all, she won. Many newborns didn't make it past their first birthday, and I often wonder if I would have survived those conditions, but I come from good stock, and something tells me I would have made it no matter what.

Stalin's reign of terror neared its end in 1951, and my grandparents were allowed to move back into their old shack in their small Aremenian village.

Chapter 8
Armenia-November, 1975

November 1975 was a monumental year in my family's life. It was the year we emigrated from Armenia to the United States. At the time, Armenia was under Russian control, and communism ruled the land.

My dad's name is Sarkis (Săr-kiss) Akhoian (ə-koy'-yen), and my mother's name is Tiroughi (Tə-roo'-gē). My parents named me after my grandfather, whose name was Hovanes (Hō-vă'-nĕs). When he moved to the United States, he shortened it to Oganes (Ō-gă-nĕs).

Just like me, my dad had abandonment issues growing up. His mother died shortly after he was born due to complications with the delivery. As you can see, my father's abandonment issues started early in his life. My father's birth was heartbreaking for my grandfather, who gained a son but lost a wife. Grandfather Oganes found it difficult raising a child in communist Armenia as a single parent. He eventually fell in love and married a woman with children from a previous marriage. Grandfather did the honorable thing and accepted his new wife's children as his own, but he abandoned my dad and uncle in the process.

My grandfather sent Sarkis to a childless family who was looking to adopt. Unable to accept his adoptive family, Sarkis decided to run away. He stowed away on a train to Yerevan, where his brother, Abraham, lived with another family. My dad was eight, and Abraham was thirteen.

Onboard the train, father managed to hide from the conductors for a few hours. He was terrified of getting caught. As an eight-year-old, he had no idea what the transit authorities would do to him. Dad hid under a seat for hours, avoiding the conductors and the other passengers. After each stop, the conductors would check the passengers for tickets. These were the most harrowing moments.

Dad's luck eventually ran out when a conductor spotted him. The man asked where his parents were, and dad lied, telling him they were in another car. The conductor took dad by the hand and said, "Show me." Dad broke free of the man's grip and ran, but there was no place to go. The man caught my father and sat him down while he called for help. Another conductor came over and interrogated my father. Dad told them the story of his adoptive parents and his need to get away. He talked about finding his brother, Abraham, and moving in with him and his new parents. The conductors must have taken pity on this eight-year-old child because they did the unexpected. They allowed Sarkis to travel to Yerevan, which was the end of the line. One of the conductors looked up Abraham's address and delivered Sarkis to him.

Abraham was young and couldn't take care of his little brother. He asked his adoptive parents if Sarkis could live with them, but they said no. Sarkis stayed with them for a couple of days until Abraham's adoptive family bought him a train ticket and sent him home. As fate would have it, my dad never saw his older brother again.

Chapter 9
Murder on Lake Imandra

I will start this chapter by talking about my Uncle Abraham, a brilliant, straight-up guy who went to school in Moscow. Abraham was on his way to doing great things, but much like me, he ran with the wrong crowd. I hope to avoid confusion in this chapter because *my* older brother's name is Abraham, and my dad's older brother was Abraham; this is his story, the story of my dad's older brother. Abraham was thirteen in the previous chapter. Fast forward six years, and he is nineteen years old.

Abraham attended the University of Moscow. He liked to party and drink in moderation, unlike many students who had no limits. One night, his friends Resad and Kerem drank heavily, and Abraham watched as they harassed a young girl. The underage girl struggled to get away, but his friends wouldn't let up. The more she tried to get away, the angrier they got. Kerem held the girl down while Resad raped her. She screamed for help, but no one came to her aid.

Sickened by what he saw, Abraham told Resad and Kerem to leave the girl alone, but they ignored him. Others at the party were too drunk to care. A few of the men even cheered while Resad raped her. Abraham stood by and did nothing to stop the assault. I'm sure he regretted it later because it was always on his mind. A few days later, Abraham confronted his friends.

"Resad," he said, "What you and Kerem did to that girl was wrong. Rape is a crime."

"Rape! Are you crazy, Abraham? We didn't rape anybody, and you saw how that girl was dressed. She was asking for it. She wanted to party with us."

"She told you and Kerem to stop, and you didn't."

"She didn't mean it, Abraham. She was drunk, we were drunk, and you were drunk, so back off, you don't really know what happened."

But Abraham didn't give up. He continued to hound, Resad and Kerem, and that caused his friends serious concern. A few days later, the men ran into Abraham in the University courtyard.

"Abraham," Kerem said, "Resad and I have been talking, and what we did to that girl was wrong, but we were hoping you would let it go this once. We didn't hurt the girl. She's probably already forgotten about it."

Abraham told them he could not forget what he saw, and the men asked for one final favor.

"Will you go fishing with us tomorrow?" Kerem asked, "We'll have a few drinks, tell a few stories, and have a few laughs. It will be just the three of us. It might be our last chance to spend time together, and then we will turn ourselves in."

Abraham agreed, and the next day, they set out on the waters of Lake Imandra. The three men loaded their gear into a fifteen-foot outboard and headed for open waters. Known for its good fishing, Imandra is 109-km long.

Three men set out on the water that day, but only two came back. When the men returned to the launch, they called the authorities and told them Abraham had fallen overboard and drowned. Lake Imandra is 220-feet at its deepest, and the authorities expected the body to surface at some point. Resad and Kerem said they tried to save Abraham, but he swallowed a lot of water and went under too quickly.

Weeks later, campers found Abraham's body on one of the islands that dot the lake. Resad and Kerem's story fell apart, and they confessed to his murder. I don't know how many years they would have gotten for raping that girl, but murder carried the death sentence.

Chapter 10
My Father-Sarkis

After returning from his train adventure, Sarkis endured another decade with his adoptive family. They were good people and took care of him, but he missed his brother and father. When he was old enough to work, Sarkis got two jobs. He got a full-time job as a crane operator and a part-time job as a taxi driver. Dad consumed himself in his work, which kept him away from his adoptive parents.

Around that time, dad fell in love and married my mother, Tiroughi. Together they had a son, my brother, Abraham. Dad worked harder now that he had a family, but he could not make any headway in the communist regime. In August of 1971, Tiroughi learned she was pregnant with me.

In 1972, my grandfather and his stepfamily moved to America, leaving Sarkis, his pregnant wife, and his grandson behind. That was Sarkis's third bout with abandonment.

On March 28, 1972, I was born. I am surprised they named me after my grandfather since he had abandoned his family, but that is the Armenian way. Later, I learned that my grandfather deeply loved Sarkis but didn't want to show it to his new wife. Grandfather never planned on abandoning his boys, and in November of 1975, he obtained a visa for all of us.

As soon as he could, my father moved us from Armenia to Hollywood, California. Hollywood might appear glitzy and glamourous to most of the world, with movie stars and movie premiers, but we never saw that side of Hollywood. We lived with my grandfather and his new family in their two-bedroom apartment because my father immigrated with no money.

The land of opportunity wasn't dishing out much when we arrived. Living with my grandfather's wife was intolerable, and we had to move out, but we didn't have much money. Dad was good with his hands, and he worked as a part-time mechanic and tow truck driver. Then he took on the job of building manager at an apartment complex. The manager's job gave him a discount on a one-bedroom, but it didn't provide an income, and living in Hollywood wasn't cheap.

Dad eventually became a long-haul truck driver. The pay was adequate, but the job deprived him of what he would later come to regret…time with his family. It also presented a problem for my mother, who managed the building with her eldest son, Abraham, while dad was away. Abraham helped with some of the repairs around the building until our father returned from his run. As for me, I was still too young to help.

I remember my parents arguing about money or the lack of money, to be more accurate. Putting food on the table and paying the bills was challenging to my parent's self-esteem. Their marriage also struggled because of the lack of money, but Armenian women are faithful to their vows, and they marry for life." For better or worse," is not taken lightly, and I respect my mother for that.

Dad eventually saved enough to buy a big rig. He became an independent owner-operator earning more money and gaining more control over his time. Eventually, he saved enough to buy a house in North Hollywood, but it took him more than ten years to do it. I work hard to achieve my goals, and I attribute some of that persistence to my father, who did what he could to provide for us.

Sarkis was a big personality; he was loud, funny, and loved by many. When he entered a room, he commanded attention. People were glad when dad walked into a bar or a party. Some would say, "And now the party begins." Dad was a handsome man whose looks were both a gift and a curse. It pains me to say this, but my father was a womanizer. Sarkis had affairs, and I despised him for that. My mother was devoted to my dad and us. She managed the building while he was away while working at a department store for the minimum wage to help with the bills. Dad was a magnet to beautiful women and had a difficult time saying no to their advances. Tiroughi knew of these affairs and stayed with him through good times and bad. I remember thinking how weak my mother was, remaining married to a cheater. I didn't have the respect or admiration for her that I have today. Today I realize that mom was dedicated to her boys first and foremost, and I love her for that.

It must have been difficult for mom when Sarkis was on the road. I am not saying my dad had a woman at every truck stop, but the thought must have haunted my mother whenever he was away. Infidelity is a selfish and cruel act. I picked up a few bad habits growing up, but I thank God infidelity was not one of them.

Part III

Redemption

Chapter 11
God Sends an Angel

It was 1990 when I first saw her at a friend's party. Her shoulder-length hair was auburn, and her face sculpted by a god. I say that now, but back then, all I could think was, *she is hot.*

I asked my friend, Jack, if he knew who she was. He told me she was single, and her name was Tamar. But Jack knew I ran with a bad crowd and told me to stay away.

"Don't waste your time, John. She comes from a good family, and if she knows half the things you've done, she'll never date you."

"Then I won't tell her what I've done," I said, "Tell her I want to meet her."

Jack walked over to Tamar and told her I thought she was beautiful and wanted to meet her. She was as cold as a winter's night, and she looked at me with what I can only describe as disdain. She told Jack she wasn't interested in meeting me and continued talking with her friends. Jack came back with the news, and I stayed away for the rest of the night, but I couldn't stop thinking about that woman. The party ended, and we went our separate ways.

A year later, I was at Benji's, the restaurant where I was arrested for road rage, when I saw Tamar again. She was eighteen, I was nineteen, and determined to date this girl. I came from a background of corruption and drugs, and she came from a good, God-fearing family. My chances of dating her were slim. I'm a pretty good salesman so, "none" wasn't part of the equation.

Tamar was with a girlfriend, Nairee, who we still see to this day, and Peter, a guy I knew from the old neighborhood. I caught Peter's attention, and he came over to our table.

"Peter," I said, "are you dating the girl with the brown hair?"

"No," he said, "she's my girlfriend's friend."

"Will you give her my number and tell her I want to meet her?

Peter walked back to his table, and I saw him pass Tamar my number. She briefly looked my way and then went back to talking with Peter and Nairee. I watched her crumble up my note and leave it on the table.

If you have learned anything about me thus far, it's that I take challenges head-on. I may have a fear of abandonment, but I don't have a fear of rejection. Tamar rejected me twice, but that didn't scare me away. I pressed Peter to get me her number, which he eventually did. I called Tamar the following day and asked her out. She agreed to lunch, but only if Caroline, a friend, could come along as a chaperone.

We met for lunch at the Elephant Bar and Grill in Burbank, California and Tamar didn't say two words the entire meal. But I remember chatting non-stop with Caroline. We talked for about two hours. Caroline convinced Tamar that I was a good guy and to give me a chance.

We started dating, and little by little, Tamar learned about my past. She was with me the night Hagop died, and she was with me for Andre's vehicular manslaughter trial, and she never wavered or left me. She was and is my strength.

I loved her parents Manuel and Rosette. They were good honest people and had done a remarkable job of raising Tamar. I wanted so badly to know what it was like to be a part of a family like that.

In Armenia, prearranged marriages are customary. The parents get together and agree that their children will wed. But this is America, and prearranged marriages aren't the norm. It was my goal to impress Tamar and her parents by proposing traditionally. I asked my aunt's husband, Gevork, to call Manuel and arrange a meeting between the two families. Usually, I would ask my father to do this, but Uncle Gevork was the closest thing I had to a dad. Gevork called Manuel and asked if the families could get together for an important discussion.

This request was code for 'John wants to marry your daughter.' Everyone knew what was coming.

I wasn't too worried about her parents saying no, because they liked me. I was now a full-time plumber with my own company, High-Quality Plumbing, and I did a lot of favors for family and friends. I bought a suit for the occasion and my brother, my mother, my aunt, uncle and I went to Tamar's house. Everyone dressed to the nines, and we brought pastries as is customary. When the time was right, uncle Gevork asked Manuel if I could have his daughter's hand in marriage. Manuel agreed, and just like that, I was engaged to this angel. Both families celebrated with dinner, wine, music, and dance. It was a night I will never forget.

We married on May 3, 1996, but the joy was short-lived. The problem was that I hadn't changed my ways. I stopped using drugs because Tamar caught me one night with a baggie of cocaine. She told me she would not be with a drug addict, but she didn't say anything about alcohol. Beer and wine weren't too hard on me, but tequila and vodka became my newest demons. I partied hard, and I am ashamed to tell you I am not a pleasant drunk. The rage I had as a teen intensified whenever I drank tequila or vodka.

On April 26, 2002, our son, Andrew, was born. You would think that the birth of a child would be a reason to stop drinking, but the opposite was true. Andrew's birth was a time of celebration for both families. My mom and my in-laws were giddy with excitement. Tamar was nurturing our baby, and I had taken on the responsibility of being a father, but I hadn't grown up.

I found myself drinking more and more with my friends, and I often came home drunk and angry at the world and my little family. Why Tamar stuck around is beyond me. But like I mentioned earlier, Armenian women are strong, loyal, and dedicated to their families. I recall days when my 3-year old son, Andrew, would hide in the closet

as I dropped a flurry of F-bombs on his mother. How I could do this to my child's mother is incomprehensible today, but I did it.
Andrew grew into a good man despite the antics of his father. Sometimes I cry thinking about that little boy having to hide from his raging father. What type of monster would do such a thing?

In 2005 we learned we were expecting our second child, Christian. When Tamar was 7-months pregnant, her parents came to visit. I had downed about half a bottle of tequila, and my rage was bubbling beneath the surface. We never read any books on parenting, and the one thing Tamar and I agreed on was not to give our kids junk food. But if you know anything about grandparents, they like to spoil the grandkids. Sometimes my mom would slip something to Andrew, maybe a piece of candy or a pastry, which bothered Tamar. We were in the living room, and Tamar told her parents a story about my mom giving Andrew some candy, which ticked me off. I never said anything negative about her parents, and I didn't appreciate her disrespecting my mother. Saying anything negative about my family was a trigger, and Tamar had just pulled it. I exploded.

My in-laws, Manuel and Rosette, were in the room when I let loose with an expulsion of obscenities. Andrew ran and hid in his room, and my wife's parents saw a side of me they didn't know I had. Rosette jumped in to defend her daughter and tried to calm me down, but that only made things worse. I walked over to the stove, picked up an iron grate, held it over my head, and threatened to throw it at my mother-in-law if she didn't f***ing leave immediately. I still remember the look of terror on Rosette's face. She told Tamar to get Andrew and leave the house with them, but Tamar didn't budge. She said this was her home, this was the life she chose, and that she wasn't going anywhere. This angel stood beside me and would not abandon me even when I was at my worst. I am ashamed to say I have thrown things at my wife, but never anything as dangerous as the iron grate I came close to throwing at her mother.

I stopped drinking that night. I have never attended an AA meeting, but I didn't touch a drop of alcohol for the next three years. Armenians like to party, and the pressure to drink is intense. I remember carrying a six-pack of non-alcoholic beer with me and taking it to parties. When someone offered me hard alcohol, I would turn them down and say I had a beer. I still drink socially. I learned that I could have a beer or a glass of wine and stop after a couple of drinks.

I don't think I would have made it without help from my brother and sister in-law, Nick and Claudia who were an integral part of my change. Tamar told them about my outburst, and these two lovely people supported Tamar and me. Nick gave me counsel when I needed it, and Claudia showed me kindness and forgiveness. They could have easily turned their backs on me, but they stood beside me, and I am forever grateful.

Tamar's parents didn't speak to us for months. I apologized a couple of days later, but Manuel didn't feel it was sincere. Six to eight months after that incident, we had a baptism for Christian. The guest list included one hundred and fifty people. My in-laws came, but it was awkward because we didn't speak, and a few of the guests noticed. Had I lost control that night and thrown that grate, I could have killed Rosette, and today I would be on death row. I don't know what stopped me, but I thank God something did.

On May 1, 2006, Christian was born. I am often astounded by some of the things we human beings do. We can tell a woman we love her one minute and cause her great pain the next. We can fall in love with a gentle family and then throw them out of our house. I remember apologizing to Tamar over and over. I took this beautiful woman as my wife and treated her and her parents like crap. All I know is the man I had become was not the man I wanted to be.

I remember praying myself to sleep that night, begging God to make me a better man. How I was able to pray in a drunken stupor is still unclear to me. That night was *the* pivotal moment in my transformation, the night I decided to change, and the night I gave my life to Christ. That was the night I made it out of hell, and who should be waiting for me on the other side? Mike West.

Chapter 12
Rooter Hero Plumbing

Had it not been for Mike West, Rooter Hero Plumbing might not exist. Mike is a third-generation plumber and one of the nicest people you will ever meet. Mike's grandfather, Jim, started Jimmie West Plumbing in 1922. Rooter Hero gets its roots from that beautiful family. Mike is a member of the Church of Jesus Christ of Latter-Day Saints. He is deeply religious and, as a young man, served his mission overseas. Mike has a great love for humanity, and I am blessed that God sent him my way.

My introduction to Mike came when my attorney, Steven Callister, told me that a friend was looking for work. Mike was going through some personal issues at the time and had to close his plumbing company. Steven told me Mike was one of the most honest people he had ever met, and he thought we should get together. I first spoke with Mike on the phone and later invited him to meet me in person. Our offices were on Lankershim Blvd., in Sun Valley, and Mike pulled up in a fire engine red, 2005 Ford Lightning pickup. His truck was so loud I thought I was at the Winter Nationals drag racing championships. I immediately liked his style.

I told Mike I wasn't looking for anyone to help me with my plumbing business but still wanted to meet with him based on Steven's recommendation. I owned a national franchise at the time, and their corporate offices provided me with plenty of help and guidance, but I told Mike that I did have an interest in starting a heating and air conditioning company. Air conditioning is a massive opportunity in Southern California. It is not unusual to have ninety-degree days in October and hit eighty-five-degree on Christmas day. Air Conditioning is not seasonal in the San Fernando Valley; it is a year-round opportunity.

With Mike's help, I built Go Green Air. The company did well, and after a few years, someone bought it from me. That put me in an odd position with Mike because he was out of work again, and I still didn't need any help with the plumbing company. I had developed such a fondness for Mike that I told him I was looking to someday get out of the franchise plumbing business and wanted my start my own company. We met several times, and together we came up with the name Rooter Hero Plumbing. Mike became president, and because of a non-compete clause in my franchise contract, I could have no involvement.

I hatched a plan that would eventually get me the company I wanted. My father-in-law had just retired, and I knew this was the perfect time to approach him with a new business proposition. I helped with the seed money, and Rooter Hero became a reality. Mike took the reins and came up with the logo, the jingle idea, and everything involving marketing. My parents-in-law were the major investors, but they stayed away and acted as silent partners.

Mike found a building in Orange County, and I donated a few empty vans and some plumbing equipment I had lying around. Mike did an incredible job of putting together a team, and Rooter Hero was on its way. Mike's business acumen and plumbing experience helped us grow quickly. He handled the training, customer complaints, and my management company dealt with the phone bookings, dispatching, and all accounting functions. Rooter Hero hired my management company to handle these items, and everything was legal and above board. The president of the franchisor was in the loop, and as long as we did everything legally, she was okay with it.

Rooter Hero was making money, and Mike continued to look for new locations. In a few years, we had grown the company to six locations, and sales were good. We had shops in San Diego, Phoenix, San Jose, Montclair, Ventura, and Orange County. Mike was involved with the day-to-day operations, but he had a personal goal that he was working toward. Mike shared that he and his wife, Diana, wanted to go to South Africa to do an 18-month mission for the Church of Jesus Christ of Latter-Day Saints.

In 2018, seven years after Rooter Hero opened its doors, I sold my national franchise and bought Rooter Hero Plumbing from my in-laws. Mike and Diana were finally free to take their missionary trip.

I remember how difficult it was getting out of my contract. I represented the largest franchises in the country and had won more awards than anyone else. The franchisor did not want to let me go because I was paying a fortune in franchise fees, but I was determined to own an independent company. Mike West was still running Rooter Hero when the franchisor sued me.

Mike and I hopped on a plane and flew to Waco, Texas, where the franchisor was based. I remember the courthouse vividly. Thirty-five stairs lead to the front door, I know because I counted them. You've heard the term dead man walking. Well, that's how I felt as I counted each step. The courthouse is painted alabaster white and is very imposing. I suppose it's painted that way to keep the oppressive heat away or, it's intended to intimidate. At the top of the building, a domed structure has a statue of Lady Justice. In her left hand, she holds the scales of justice and a sword in her right hand. What I couldn't see was the blindfold that signifies that justice is blind. I wouldn't swear that she didn't have on a blindfold, but I couldn't see it. It's funny the things you notice just before your execution. I wondered if the sword meant that Mike and I were about to be skewered.

It didn't take long for me to understand why the blindfold might have been missing. My franchise contract had a provision that forced us to use a local Texas attorney to represent us. I had to leave our attorney, who knew everything about our case in Los Angeles. I told Mike that it seemed like we were walking into a pit of quicksand, and our new attorney wasn't about to throw us a rope. To make things worse, the court scheduled the mediation over Valentine's Day, which meant that Mike and I wouldn't get to spend time with our wives. I remember being in that hallway waiting for the bailiff to call our names. I paced up and down but then decided to sit. I didn't want them to see me sweat. I sat on a hard wooden bench, looked at Mike, and wondered how we had gotten into this mess.

The judge put us in one room and the Waco team in another. The judge went back and forth with offers and counteroffers. He didn't let any of us break for lunch, and at 5 o'clock, the air conditioning in the building automatically turned off. The judge wouldn't let us leave. I guess he'd done this before because his tactics were working. There were no vending machines on the floor, and we were hungry and sweating. We were $500,000 apart, and it didn't seem like we were going to settle when Mike West pulled me aside. "John," he said, "500,000 dollars is a lot of money, but what is it worth to you to be done with this thing and get on with your life?"

There is a lot of wisdom in what Mike said. Sometimes our egos get the better of us. Mike made me realize that winning was subjective. The real question was, what was I willing to pay for peace of mind, less anxiety, and the chance to own a company with no strings attached? To me, winning my case meant paying a total of $500,000 and no more. Waco was asking for 1,000,000. I was focused on numbers and not what was really at stake, which was my happiness and health. I thought long and hard on what Mike said, agreed to pay the $1,000,000, got out of my contract with Waco, and treated Mike to a nice dinner.

I never realized what a heavy burden I was carrying until I made it disappear. The ordeal was at long last over. There were no more attorneys to pay, no more franchise fees, and no more Waco, Texas. I tell myself the money I spent was worth it, and going to court was all part of my journey because Rooter Hero is doing well, my family is doing well, and Mike and Diana are happy in retirement.

When we started Rooter Hero Plumbing, I had just begun my sobriety, and I was looking for guidance. Some of my organization's hardest working and loyal people were from the Church of Jesus Christ of Latter-Day Saints. I knew that Mike was an elder in his church, and I turned to him for advice. These employees were some of the nicest people I had ever met, and I asked Mike what the secret was. He told me about how these young men go on missions and how they follow the word of God. Mike invited me to attend a couple of services at his church, and I found the experience enlightening. I thought – what a great way to raise children.

I was baptized Christian, but my parents only attended church on Easter and Christmas. With the Church of Jesus Christ, I found myself attending regularly. Things were going well in my life, and I considered becoming a member of the church. I sat down to talk with one of the elders, who told me he didn't think I was ready. I appreciated his honesty because he was not interested in converting me but in helping me. He asked if my family would support my baptism into the new church, and my answer was no. I had been attending services on my own, and my family thought that I was crazy or going through a phase.

"We are in the business of bringing families together," the elder said, "not tearing them apart." As important as the teachings of the church were to me, I was on my own. My wife and boys were not interested in attending services and told me it was my journey. I switched to my local Armenian Evangelical church, where my family would occasionally attend with me. God's message is universal when you're ready to receive it.

Mike West still wasn't done with me. He asked if I lived by a code of values, and I told him I did not. Mike handed me a pamphlet that talked about gratitude, family, friends, honesty, and integrity. "These are the values I live by," Mike said, "feel free to read it." That pamphlet had a transformational effect on my life. Much of the credit for my change goes to Mike, who helped me become a better man.

Chapter 13
Service Titan

I have wronged many people in my life, some of whom I knew and others whose faces are a blur. I have apologized to many of these good people, and I have made amends. I cannot undo some of the things I've done, but I can start anew. Part of my transformation was to take the focus off of me and to focus on helping others.

Rooter Hero Plumbing works with countless charities throughout the year. We help feed and clothe the less fortunate, deliver Christmas trees and presents to underprivileged children, and we give people looking for a second chance, a second chance.

My most significant contribution to the plumbing industry came when I unknowingly entered the world of cyberspace. Long before I got out of my franchise contract, my company was having software problems. In 2010 we were using software that helped dispatch plumbers to our client's homes. The software was basic and wasn't providing the information or service we needed. I looked at another software company but found them inflexible. I asked for specific features to help us serve our customers better, and their answer was always no. They believed their software was perfect, and they had no intention of listening to their customers, who were desperately trying to provide input.

I had a laundry list of things I needed our software to do, and as I mentioned earlier, none of the companies had an interest in helping me out. At the suggestion of a friend, I met with two young men, Vahe Kuzoyan and Ara Mahdessian, who said they could do everything I requested. The name of their company was Linx Logic, and they were anxious to please. I was so excited by their enthusiasm and knowledge that I invested in their dream by becoming a customer and by helping them improve their product. What follows is their story.

In 2009, Vahe earned his computer science degree from the University of Southern California. While at USC, Vahe started an Armenian club of which he was president. Vahe was a big fan of networking, and he suggested the club put together a retreat in Big Bear, California, and invite members of other Armenian clubs to join them. Invites went out to other colleges and universities. Ara Mahdessian was attending Stanford University when he saw the invitation. Ara's first thought was that there were going to be a lot of beautiful Armenian women at the retreat, and so he RSVP'd immediately. Little did he realize that this trip would change his life.

Vahe bumped into Ara in the lobby, and the two hit it off immediately. They stayed in touch, and a couple of months later, an opportunity arose. Stanford was holding a contest looking for the best software idea of the year. Ara knew Vahe had put together a basic software program for his uncle, who was a contractor. He called Vahe and asked if he could come to Stanford and help his team put together a similar program for the contest. Vahe didn't hesitate and was on the next flight to Palo Alto. When the two men reunited, the first thing they did was party. They had a memorable weekend, and on Sunday night, just before packing it in, the men realized they hadn't spent a minute on the project, which was due the following day.

At 2:00 AM, with horrible hangovers, the men got to work. The assignment was haphazardly done, but at least Ara and his team had something to turn in. Vahe flew home, and before the week was over, he got a call from Ara.

"Vahe, you won't believe what happened."

"What?" Vahe asked.

"We won first place."

"You're kidding. We threw that thing together in four hours."

"That tells me there must be something valuable here," Ara said, "Why don't we develop this further and see if we can sell it."

I met with Vahe and Ara, who wanted my business and asked if I could introduce them to the franchisor I was working with to see if they could pitch their software to other franchisees. I gave them my word that I would make it happen. At the time, the plumbing franchise had over three thousand members. I told the two men that I would become their biggest supporter and would tell everyone about them.

When I met Vahe and Ara, our company used Plumbingware (not real name), a software program the franchisor wanted us to use. The program was slow, bulky, and did not support the franchisee. It was just another way for the franchisor to make more money. I tried to drop that program, but my contract bound me. The program recorded every sale so the franchisor could keep track of its royalties. That was not a problem. The problem was that the software didn't help us expedite technicians to peoples' homes.

I asked Vahe and Ara if there was a way to tie Plumbingware and Linx Logic together. Connecting the two programs would allow me to use the best of Lynx Logic while not breaking my contract with the franchisor. They said yes to every request I made. Linx Logic was so superior to Plumbingware that I asked the brass from Waco to come to Los Angeles to see a presentation. When the franchisor arrived, they took over the meeting and did a sales pitch for Plumbingware in front of Vahe and Ara. The two men never got to show what they had. The meeting was a complete bust.

Frustrated by how Waco treated them, I contacted a friend who bought his franchise when I purchased mine. Kurt was a very outspoken franchisee who did not seem to like anything Waco management was doing. I asked Kurt what his biggest challenge was and, he said it was Plumbingware. Although Kurt ran a small franchise operation, he was very outspoken, and Waco considered him a pain in their side. Kurt would stir the pot at company events and gatherings by telling other franchisees everything the franchisor was doing wrong.

Waco was getting so many complaints about Plumbingware, that they finally agreed to review several programs to see if they could satisfy their franchisees. Linx Logic was one of ten programs that Waco planned to review. I promised Vahe and Ara that I would be their biggest cheerleader, and I was determined to keep my word. Since I was the biggest franchisee in the country, people listened to me, and all I could talk about was Linx Logic. In an attempt to quash the uprising, Waco agreed to let Kurt use Linx Logic on a trial basis. Waco's reasoning, we found out later, was that since Kurt never seemed to be happy with anything, he would tear Linx Logic apart, which meant Waco could continue to promote Plumbingware.

Kurt fell in love with Linx Logic and refused to use Plumbingware any longer. He contacted other franchisees, and the next thing Waco knew, most of the franchisees were demanding to use Linx Logic. Waco knew they had to take Linx Logic seriously, but they wanted to see their operation before approving the software.

Vahe and Ara were working out of Vahe's dad's office in Glendale, California. The entire room was less than five hundred square feet, and they knew Waco would not be impressed with a couple of guys sharing an office with Vahe's dad. The men took out a thirty-day lease on a thousand square foot office. They rented desks, office chairs, whiteboards, wall monitors, and artwork. They purchased seventeen iPads and then recruited seventeen friends to fill the office and pretend to work while the brass from Waco toured the facility.

The office was impressive, and the "employees" seemed engaged in their "work." Employees were passing iPads back and forth and appeared to be involved in serious discussions. Waco's management walked away wholly impressed, and they invited Vahe and Ara to make a formal presentation to the brass in Waco. The presentation blew the other companies out of the water, and Linx Logic got the account.

Later, when Vahe and Ara asked their friends what they were doing on the iPads, they found out they were having a tic-tac-toe tournament. Luckily, the Waco brass never bothered to ask what the employees were working on. Today Linx Logic is known as Service Titan. It provides software to thousands of companies in the service industry, including plumbing, electrical, heating and air, and pest control.

I learned later on from Vahe that he was in discussions with Ara about shutting the company down and going their separate ways. This happened a month or two before they got the franchise contract. I wonder how different today's service industry would be if it had not been for that single 3000 franchise contract. It was a miracle that they went from talking about splitting up and doing something different to a $10.5 billion valuation. Service Titan changed the service industry and improved the lives of so many owners in the trades. I would like to think that those early day efforts helped put this technology company on the map.

I am honored to have had a part in the Service Titan success story. After the turmoil of my teenage years, it was time to give back and help others. Vahe, Ara, and I remain close friends, and I continue to sing their praises.

Chapter 14
Brotherhood

As you might recall, my dad's brother, Abraham, was murdered while attending school in Russia. But my dad had a stepbrother, whom we never really got to know. Not knowing uncle Grigor has left a void in my life.

I never knew uncle Grigor, and my kids don't know their uncle Abraham. My brother is estranged from my family. Funny how we lived in that same tiny apartment in North Hollywood for thirteen years, and now we don't even talk. Abraham and I worked together for a short time, and then as we each got married, we grew apart. I've tried to figure out why we don't talk, and I think a lot of it comes down to competition. Abraham and I are similar in that we are competitive. My mother would often compare our successes, and that didn't help. Like me, Abraham started his own plumbing company and is successful in his own right.

In an earlier chapter, I mentioned that success is subjective. Abraham has a good marriage, a solvent and profitable company, and he is a good provider. He is happy, something I missed out on for many years. I wish we could stop comparing bank accounts and get back to what's important – loving each other.

I fear that my boys will carry on this terrible tradition and grow apart as adults. My wife and I agreed never to compare them to each other. The only thing we want for them is happiness. I pray that they will remain close, get together with their families on holidays and break bread.

I am an uncle in name only. My nephews don't know me, and my boys don't know their Uncle Abe or first cousins. I have done a lot to fix myself, but some things remain broken. I still live in a fractured family structure, but promise to do what I can to resolve things before running out of time.

Wedding Photo.
Happy times.

Andrew's
Baptism.

Christian's baptism. These were difficult times as you can see on our faces. I wasn't speaking to my in-laws at this time.

My Uncle Abraham who was murdered at Lake Imranda.

Tamar and my favorite dog in front of
our North Hollywood house.

My first plumbing truck. High Quality Plumbing

Abraham at the piano and me on the guitar. My dad used to love having music in the house. We took a lot of music lessons and sadly no longer play.

Pasha and Rayel
my great
grandparents who
were taken from
their home at
gunpoint and
exiled to Siberia.

Me and my 280Z, the car in which I drove my aunt to my juvenal court hearing.

This is the motorcycle my dad was helping me with when he had his fatal heart attack. This is our backyard in North Hollywood.

In Armenia posing with orphans we supported. We sent them hundreds of pairs of shoes, and hygienic essentials.

Family Photo 2021
L-R Tamar, Andrew, Christian, and I.

Part IV

Giving Back-Making Amends

Chapter 15
Fund Raiser-July, 2021

A ten-year-old child watches his father strike his mother. He thinks nothing of it because domestic violence is a regular occurrence in Armenia. It is the life that thousands of Armenian children and women experience every day. The child, dirty and hungry, is destined to live and relive this horrific cycle. His house is decrepit and run down. He is uneducated, and his chance of escaping this predestined life of domestic violence diminishes with every birthday. This child and his mother are shackled to a life of poverty and physical brutality.

I am hosting an opulent poker party. Strings of lights adorn our backyard, where a one-hundred-and-eighty-degree panoramic view of the San Fernando Valley beguiles my guests. A private chef prepares a meal most people in Armenia will never savor. An outdoor music system plays gently in the background. The green felt of the poker table holds thousands of dollars in gaming chips.

"I'm all in," I say as I push my stack of chips to the middle of the table.

"I'll call," another says.

"Straight to the King." I turn my hole cards.

"Beats me," he says. The dealer pushes the chips in my direction. I have just won $8000 in play money. "How was the food?" I ask another player at the table.

It was fantastic." I step away from the table, asking the thirty people in my home for a few minutes of their time. A karaoke machine doubles as a microphone. I tap the mike and blow on it to make sure it's working.

It takes a minute for everyone to settle in. I continue tapping on the microphone until everyone quiets down enough for me to speak. I am not comfortable talking in front of large groups, but I stay focused on the reason for this gathering and overcome my insecurity.

"In 1988," I start "a major earthquake devastated Armenia. People from all over the world joined efforts to help the victims, and my father was among those who went back to Armenia to lend a hand. He brought back disturbing videos and pictures of the destruction, and as a 15-year-old kid, I still remember thinking that I would like to help people one day as my father did. I remember wanting to give hope to thousands of children and rebuild that beautiful country. A year after my dad's trip, he fell and died in front of me.

Last week I went to my mom's house for our weekly dinner, and she said, "Next Thursday is your Dad's thirty-second death anniversary. Do you want to go to the cemetery with me?"

"Mom, I can't go to the cemetery, I said, "because I am hosting a fundraiser at the house, we are raising money for a small village in Armenia that needs a school, and I have a lot of work to do."

My mother smiles. "Your Dad would be proud of what you're doing."

When we planned this day, I didn't realize it fell on my father's death anniversary. My mom said, "It is God's Will to make this happen. You will have a very successful fundraiser."

I look around the room filled with successful Armenian business people who are grateful to live in America. I continue with my speech. "First of all, I want to thank all of you who showed up today to support this worthy cause. All donations collected will go toward the development of a new Smart Center in Armivor, Armenia. I am personally pledging $25,000 tonight. Who will join me?"

One by one, hands sprout like corn stalks around the room, "Let's make these donations as big as possible for the kids living in this village who don't have access to the technology our kids have. Let's help them so they can gain knowledge and skills to better the future of their country. Haig told me that we would have a wall dedicated to all of you who are here tonight. Because you are the ones making this possible, every one of you will have their names on the school's Wall of appreciation.

Haig Boyadijian is the energetic Senior Director of Development for The Children of Armenia Fund (COAF). His smile is contagious as he takes the microphone. "Ladies and Gentlemen, thank you for participating in this five-thousand-dollar-a plate meal. We should applaud our sushi chef for his efforts. We should also applaud John Akhoian and his family for organizing this event, lending us their home, and inviting all of you fine people. In my experience," he continues, "There are two types of donors in this world—those who need a tax break and who support causes with their donations. And then there's John, who came from humble and difficult beginnings and wants to make a difference. Charities cannot survive without both types, but I want to acknowledge John and his family for suggesting this fundraiser. Thanks to John and each one of you, we raised a lot of money tonight. The dollar is strong in Armenia, and this money will get the project started. You are the first to donate, and thanks to you, we are well on our way to building a Smart Center where we can educate children and build hope for the future of Armenia."

Chapter 16
The Nagorno-Karabakh War-2020

In September of 2020, Covid-19 was ravaging the world. In the United States, businesses closed, schools closed, people wore masks, and socially distanced. Millions were infected, and hospitals overrun.

In Armenia, the landscape was different. On September 27[th,] war broke out. It was a battle between Azerbaijan, influenced by Turkey, and the Republic of Artsakh, part of Armenia. The war left thousands dead on both sides, and hundreds of Armenians were captured and abused as prisoners of war in Azerbaijan. Meanwhile, oblivious to territorial boundaries, the virus continued its march across the continent. Both sides worked tirelessly and ultimately agreed to a cease-fire. Under the agreement, Armenia said it would return some of the territories it held since 1994.

In my opinion, the world turned its back on Armenia with the genocide and again with the 2020 war. The humiliation the Armenian people endured has caused generational trauma. Armenians are resilient and will do whatever they can to provide for their families. I am blessed with a successful company and the ability to help those less fortunate. We raised money to support the war effort. We helped provide helmets, bulletproof vests, and other life-saving equipment.

***

In 2021 Haig came to me and told me about a particular project. "John," Haig said, "we are $38,000 short of building a gymnasium. These children are suffering, and they need to know what it's like to be a kid. They need to play, and laugh, and escape the trauma they will undoubtedly face when they get home."

I have always wanted to build a project that will serve generations of Armenians. My boys need to know that our money can make a difference, but I do not easily part with $38,000. I asked a friend in Armenia to look at the project and to give me his opinion as to whether I should donate the money or not. He called me back and said, "You need to jump all in. This project is worthwhile, and if $38,000 will complete it, it's well worth it."

COAF was grateful for the donation, and they offered to mount a plaque with my family's name on it. I asked if they would put my father's name on it instead. The plaque now proudly displays the words, *This gym was built in the name of Sarkis Akhonian.*

Chapter 17
The Armenian Genocide

The year is 1915; the place: Turkey. A husband buries his wife and daughter up to their necks in the sand in an act of mercy. The women will starve, or their lungs will collapse from the weight of the earth, or their faces will burn in the sun, but they beg their husbands to do this as a way to avoid rape. It is an unthinkable predicament faced by thousands of Armenians looking for a way to survive the horror of the 1915 genocide.

I donate time and money to Armenian children and families based on my mother and father's telling me about the Armenian genocide. I have a never-ending love for the United States. This great country sheltered and harbored my family, but I cannot stop thinking of those we left behind.

A dozen families huddle in a Turkish cave. Parents place their hands over their babies' mouths, stifling their hungry cries, praying the Turks will not find them. Outside, tree branches block the mouth of the cave. Turks pile the branches high and light the dry tinder and leaves. A bonfire erupts, obliterating the only egress. Inside, smoke fills the cavern, making it impossible for the huddled masses to breathe.

A businessman in Armenia contacts me. He has heard of some of the work I do with schools in the area. He is desperate to provide jobs for his village and asks if he can make a business proposal. This gentleman employs twenty young Armenian adults who hold master's degrees and cannot earn enough money to provide for their families. His employees speak perfect English, and he hopes we will consider using them as call center agents. Unwilling to let my current staff go, I propose a trial period where they can answer our calls after our regular business hours. The experiment fails because the Armenian agents misunderstand some of our slang, jargon, and idioms. I cancel the trial but give them leads that might help develop their business.

Armenian Christians are driven from their homeland by Turkish Muslims. The Turks deport, starve, burn and shoot more than one million Armenians. The final count will reach 1.5 million Armenians murdered at the hands of the Turks. This tragedy gets buried in history when Hitler's troops sent six million Jews to their deaths. Before his death, Hitler would say, 'no one will remember the Armenian genocide after what I have done.'

I owe it to my ancestors to keep the memory of the Armenian genocide alive. I cannot allow their death and suffering to go unnoticed. I hope Hitler chokes on those words as he inhales the fire and brimstone of hell.

Epilogue

The title of this book, *Temporarily Broken*, does not mean I consider myself fixed, far from it. Am I on the mend? Yes!.

In my teenage years, I was rudderless. My father, the disciplinarian in the family, was absent in my life, and I gravitated to people who valued drugs and corruption. My friends and their bad habits represented my entire world. I didn't know of another way to act until I met my wife and her family. Even then, it took that one terrible night to shake me to my core.

Am I fixed? Heck, no. I still need to repair the relationship between my brother and me, and I still need to repair certain business relationships. I believe some of my broken pieces have been recovered and glued back together, but they still don't look like the person I want to be.

As much as I loved Hagop, Tatul, Andre, and my other childhood friends, their choices negatively impacted me. Thankfully they no longer influence my life choices. I used to listen to my friends, and now I listen to self-help audiobooks and read the bible. My new mentors are authors and motivational speakers. I want to acknowledge those who now shape my life, such as Jim Rohn, Zig Ziglar, Brian Tracy, Darren Hardy, Brian Buffini, Tom Hopkins, and others – too numerous to mention. My mentors include my coaches and pastors Don, Dan, Lee, Jeff, Jason, Haig, Ron, and Joel. Thank you for being there when I need you.

I want to thank my co-workers and associates who participate with me in a weekly book club. We read positive books and discuss how they can improve our lives, which has made a big difference.

Recently, my friend Nor invited my wife and me to join him, his wife and a few other couples for a weekend in Napa. Besides the beauty of the land, what struck me most was the story of how fine wines are made. Grapes that undergo no stress and have an easy growing cycle produce good wines, but the truly fine wines come from grapes that endure stress, dehydration, extreme heat, and cold. These grapes are the survivors. They have character, and that leads to a great-tasting wine.

While on that walking tour, I reflected on my life; the near-death experiences, the losses, the struggles, and ultimately the victories

As I end this book, I have some final thoughts for my sons and anyone reading it.

My goal in writing this book is for my boys to see the WARNING signs that I did not see. I made many mistakes in my life, and I hope that they will serve as examples of what not to do. I hope that the second half of my book lays out examples of what to do. I made course corrections along the way and did things that benefited my life and others. I hope you can use these examples to improve your life. I am proudest of my two boys, my wife, and the life we share.

There are six points I want to leave you with:

1. I plan to live in faith, knowing a Greater power is guiding me. I plan on keeping this faith as my life's foundation. I will pray daily and ask God for the forgiveness of my sins and ask for wisdom.
2. I plan to live a long life by eating right, exercising, and feeding my mind with positive thoughts. As strange as this may sound, I plan to live to age 137. I can't prevent a tragedy or an accident; however, I can extend my life by making healthy choices. I want to live long enough to see my family grow: to see my grandkids and great-grandkids. I also want to be the catalyst to help my family make the good choices to live a long and healthy life.
3. I plan on a lifelong marriage with my wife, Tamar. I want to spend the rest of my life being married to this incredible woman. As you learned from earlier chapters, she has made a tremendous contribution to my

life, changing me for the better. I plan on being a great husband and friend.

4. I want to be here for you boys, and I want to set a good example as a father. I want you to know that you can come to me for guidance, and I want to see you make good decisions to become successful in every area of your life. My relationship with you is important to me. You have been the driving force in my growth as a father. I want to share life experiences like skiing, mountain biking, hiking, reading, taking trips, etc. I want to be there for you – something I wanted for myself but didn't get because my dad died.

5. I am committed to becoming the best in my industry. Work hard and build the largest plumbing empire in the world. I am willing to work as long and as hard as it takes to accomplish that goal. I want to work until the very end. I don't ever want to retire. When my time comes, and God calls on me, I want to be fully active as I am today.

6. I want to give to others who are less fortunate. I plan to give half of my wealth to the greater good one day. I want to be known as a giver, not a taker. None of us are going to take our wealth with us. Understand this early and start giving. You will be much happier while helping others.

My life has been a roller coaster ride with a lot of highs and lows. I am writing this book at age 49. The roller coaster has not slowed down, but the ups and downs are gentler. That is because I make better decisions than I did in my early years. If I can leave you with a final thought, it's never to stop improving. Life gets better as you get better.